P9-DNK-498

Good Question!

Why Does Earth Spin?
AND OTHER QUESTIONS ABOUT . . .
Our Planet

STERLING CHILDREN'S BOOKS
New York

STERLING CHILDREN'S BOOKS
New York

An Imprint of Sterling Publishing
387 Park Avenue South
New York, NY 10016

STERLING CHILDREN'S BOOKS and the distinctive Sterling Children's Books logo are trademarks of Sterling Publishing Co., Inc.

Text © 2014 by Mary Kay Carson
Illustrations © 2014 by Sterling Publishing Co, Inc.

Photo Credits: Alamy © RIA Novosti: 27; Getty Images © National Geographic Creative: 30; iStockphoto.com © IBorisoff: 15; © pjmorley: 22; © shaunl: 20; © t_kimura: 2, 3, 9, 10, 16, 21, 24, 26, 27, 31, 32; © teekid: 22, 26, 27, 30 (tape); © Akbar Nemati via sxc.hu: 26

All rights reserved. No part of this publication may be reproduced, stored in a retrieval system, or transmitted in any form or by any means (including electronic, mechanical, photocopying, recording, or otherwise) without prior written permission from the publisher.

ISBN 978-1-4549-0674-2 [hardcover]
ISBN 978-1-4549-0675-9 [paperback]

Library of Congress Cataloging-in-Publication Data

Carson, Mary Kay, author.
 Why does Earth spin? : and other questions about our planet / Mary Kay Carson.
   pages cm. -- (Good question)
 Audience: K-3.
 Includes bibliographical references and index.
 ISBN 978-1-4549-0675-9 (paperback) -- ISBN 978-1-4549-0674-2 (hardcover) 1. Earth (Planet)--Miscellanea--Juvenile literature. I.
Title. II. Series: Good question!
 QB631.4.C378 2014
 525--dc23
                                                                                                    2013019123

Distributed in Canada by Sterling Publishing
c/o Canadian Manda Group, 165 Dufferin Street
Toronto, Ontario, Canada M6K 3H6
Distributed in the United Kingdom by GMC Distribution Services
Castle Place, 166 High Street, Lewes, East Sussex, England BN7 1XU
Distributed in Australia by Capricorn Link (Australia) Pty. Ltd.
P.O. Box 704, Windsor, NSW 2756, Australia

Design by Andrea Miller
Paintings by Peter Bull

For information about custom editions, special sales, and premium and corporate purchases, please contact
Sterling Special Sales at 800-805-5489 or specialsales@sterlingpublishing.com.

Manufactured in China
Lot #:
4 6 8 10 9 7 5 3
06/15

www.sterlingpublishing.com/kids

CONTENTS

Where is planet Earth?

Each star in the night sky is a giant ball of hot, fiery gases. The sun is a star, too. Earth is a planet that circles around, or orbits, the sun. A planet is a huge sphere, or ball, that orbits a star. Planets and everything else that travels around a star—moons, asteroids, and comets—make up a solar system. Our solar system has the sun at its center. The sun is one of billions of stars in our galaxy, the Milky Way. The Milky Way is one of billions of galaxies in the universe.

Earth isn't the closest or farthest planet from the sun. It is not the biggest or smallest planet, either. Eight planets orbit the sun. Mercury, Venus, Earth, and Mars are the closest planets to the sun. They are all rocky, terrestrial planets, which means their surfaces are hard and solid. All four terrestrial planets, including Earth, have mountains, valleys, and volcanoes. The other four planets are made of gases and mushy liquids with no solid land. Jupiter, Saturn, Uranus, and Neptune are cold, gassy planets far from the sun. Earth is the third planet from the sun. It circles the sun between Venus and Mars. Venus is hotter than Earth, and Mars is colder. From space, Earth looks like a small blue marble because most of its surface is covered by water.

How big is Earth?

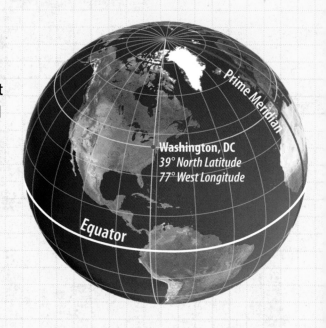

Washington, DC
39° North Latitude
77° West Longitude

Prime Meridian

Equator

Earth is small for a planet. On Jupiter, there is a hurricane-like storm three times bigger than Earth! Earth is only the fifth largest planet in our solar system, but it is the biggest terrestrial planet. More than a dozen Mercury-sized planets could fit inside Earth. Venus is closest to Earth in size. The distance all the way around Earth's middle, its circumference, is about 24,900 miles, or 40,000 kilometers (40,000 km). Venus's circumference is about 1,250 miles (2,012 km) shorter. As a comparison, if Earth were the size of a basketball, Venus would be the size of a soccer ball.

Where on Earth are you?

Earth may be a small planet, but it's a big place. The surface of Earth covers nearly 197 million square miles (510 million square kilometers). To make it easier to locate and describe specific places on Earth, we use a system of imaginary lines that form a grid.

Latitude lines go across and circle Earth. The most famous line of latitude is the equator, which wraps around Earth's middle. Lines of latitude start at 0 degrees (°) at the equator and go up to 90° north and down to 90° south. Lines of longitude run up and down between Earth's poles. The most famous line of longitude is the prime meridian. Longitude lines start at 0° at the prime meridian and then go 180° around west and 180° east. Any location can be described by a combination of longitude and latitude lines. The position of Washington, DC, is 39° N, 77° W. This means it is 39 degrees north of the equator and 77 degrees west of the prime meridian.

Earth is tiny compared to Jupiter, the largest planet in our solar system. But Earth is big compared to miniature Mercury.

Jupiter

Earth

Mercury

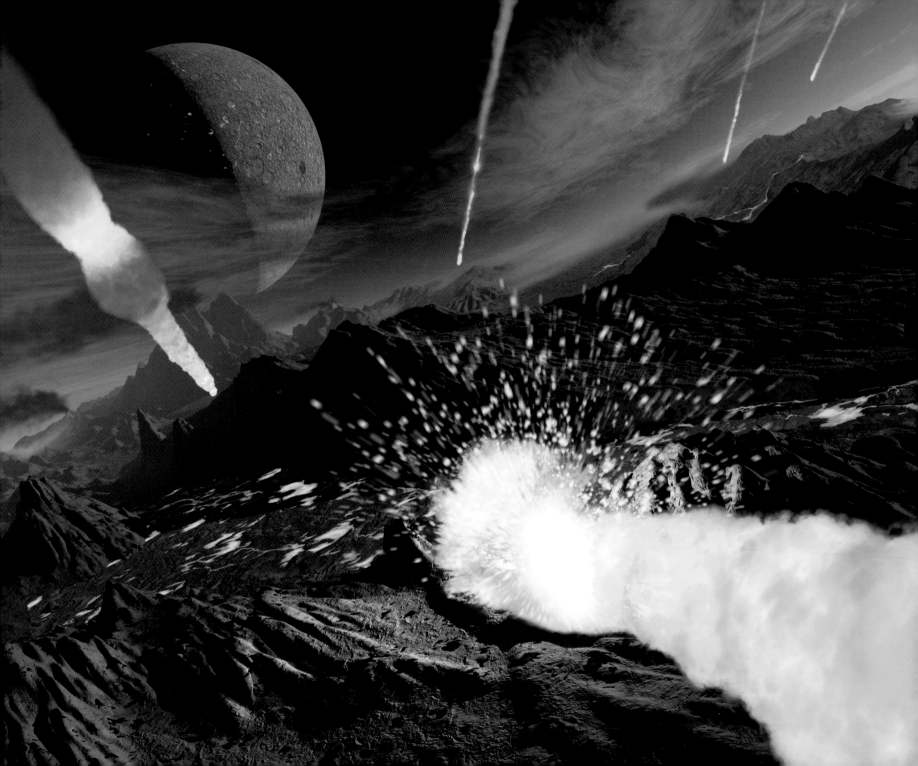

How old is our planet?

Our whole solar system, including Earth, formed from a cloud of dust and gas about 4½ billion years ago. That's a long time, but Earth has gone through a lot of changes over its history. Early Earth was a nightmarish place. Asteroids and comets from space pounded the planets. Those giant rocks were leftovers from the solar system's formation. They covered Earth and the moon with craters. On Earth, volcanoes across the planet spewed out seas of lava that melted and re-formed the land again and again. Volcanic eruptions released lots of toxic gases. Because of the asteroids falling from the sky, the high temperatures, and the poisonous gases, humans could not have survived on Earth when it was a young planet. After billions of years, plants and simple life-forms created enough oxygen to change Earth's atmosphere. Only then did the planet become liveable for humans and other animals.

Why does Earth spin?

The solar system formed out of swirling gas, circling rocks, and spinning space dust and debris. Planets were formed when some of that spinning space material clumped together into balls. The new planets continued to spin as they were formed and never stopped spinning. A planet spins around an imaginary line through its center called an axis. Every 24 hours our planet completes one spin on its axis. For some of those hours Earth is facing the sun. As our planet keeps turning, the sun sets where you are and day turns to night.

If Earth is spinning, why don't we feel like we're on an amusement park ride? Because everything else on Earth is moving, too. You don't feel the speed any more than you do while riding in a car. The cookie you're eating in a car that's moving at 60 miles per hour (97 kilometers per hour) doesn't seem like it is moving. Why not? Because everything else—your hand, mouth, and car seat—is moving at 60 miles per hour, too.

What is Earth made of?

As Earth was forming, it heated up and its insides melted. Heavy materials in the melted rock sank toward Earth's center. Lighter materials floated up to the top. This created layers inside Earth that still exist.

If you drilled down about 3,960 miles (6,370 km), you'd reach the very center of Earth. This is Earth's core, a ball of mostly iron and nickel. The metals are so squashed by the weight of the planet above them that they are squeezed into a solid inner core. Temperatures here range from 8,000 degrees Fahrenheit (8,000°F) to 12,000°F, or 4,450 degrees Celsius (4,450°C) to 6,650°C. Surrounding the solid inner core is the outer core. It is also made of metals, but they are less solid and more like a liquid. The next layer is the mantle. More than half of all the material making up Earth is in its middle mantle layer. The deepest part of the mantle is about 1,800 miles (2,900 km) below the surface. The mantle is a vast layer of hot, mushy melted rock that's moving.

The top layer is what you stand on, the crust. Compared with the mantle, it's an astonishingly thin layer, like an egg's shell or the skin of an apple. Earth's crust is thicker under land and thinner under the oceans. The rocks and minerals that make up the ocean floor and dry land are part of the crust. The crust of the continents is ten times older than the ocean crust. Scientists have found rocks in Australia that are 4 billion years old.

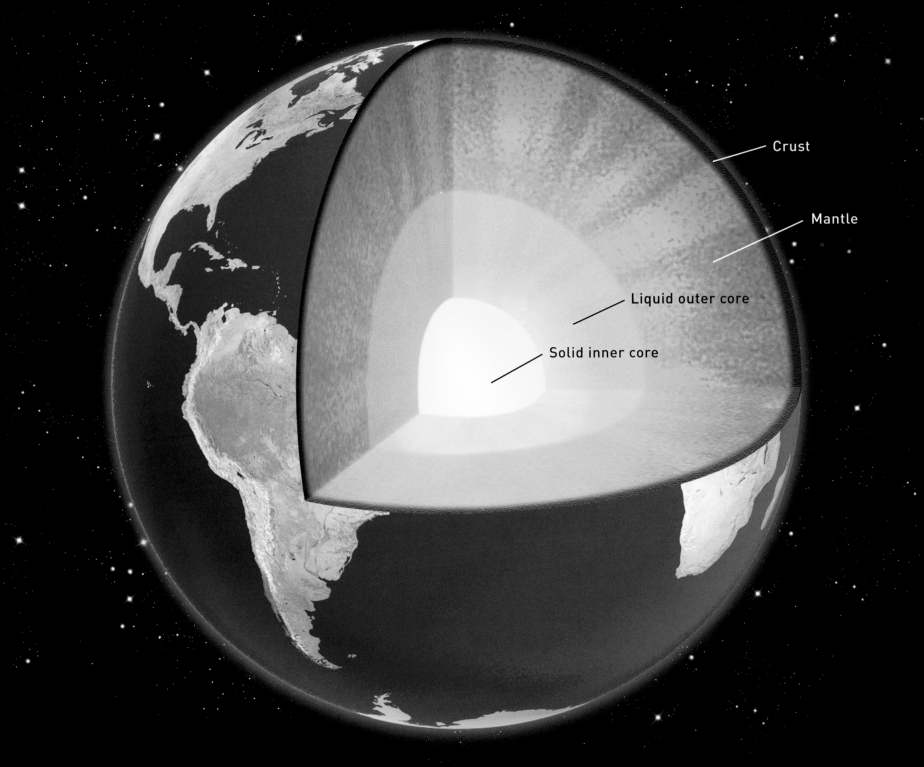

Crust

Mantle

Liquid outer core

Solid inner core

Mountains are made by clashing tectonic plates. As plates shove into each other and up and over one another, rock is pushed up into a *growing* mountain range.

Mountain range

Crust

Tectonic plate

Tectonic plate

Mantle

Does Earth move under our feet?

Earth's thin rocky crust is not connected to the layer below it. The crust just floats on top of the mantle, like crackers float on soup. The mushy rock of the mantle sinks down and rises up in slow flowing waves. The mantle's constant churning moves the crust floating on top of it, too. It breaks up the crust into big chunks. Earth's crust is broken up into about a dozen big pieces called tectonic plates. They fit together like puzzle pieces.

The ever-moving mantle scoots and drags the tectonic plates around the planet. Some of the faster plates move as much as 6 inches (15 centimeters) a year. Whatever is on top of the tectonic plates goes along with it. This is why the continents have changed their shape and position. About 250 million years ago, there was only a single continent, Pangea. It was a giant supercontinent. Over time, the moving tectonic plates broke up Pangea into today's seven continents—Antarctica, North America, South America, Africa, Australia, Asia, and Europe. In another 250 million years the continents will have drifted far enough to end up together again!

Clashing tectonic plates make for lots of action. Earthquakes, volcanoes, tsunamis, mountain-making, and seafloor spreading all happen where plates clash. It's the way Earth recycles its crust, makes new rocks, and changes its surface.

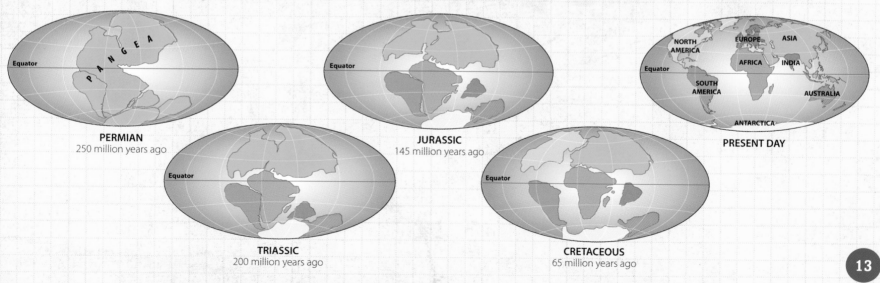

PERMIAN
250 million years ago

TRIASSIC
200 million years ago

JURASSIC
145 million years ago

CRETACEOUS
65 million years ago

PRESENT DAY

How much of our planet is covered in water?

Earth is an ocean planet. Seawater at least 2½ miles (4 km) deep covers 70 percent of Earth's surface. If Earth's surface were cut into ten even chunks, seven would be ocean. Mountains, forests, volcanoes, deserts, jungles, lakes, and rivers make up the other 30 percent of Earth's surface. Most of Earth's water is salty seawater. If all the water in the oceans disappeared, the layer of salt left behind would be as thick as half a football field. Freshwater is rare. If all Earth's water fit into a gallon jug, only about one-half cup of it would be freshwater.

Water is amazing stuff. It's the only natural substance that can exist as a liquid, a solid, and a gas at Earth's temperatures. Solid water, or ice, melts into liquid water on a sunny afternoon. Puddles of liquid water evaporate into water vapor, a gas. Water's special properties constantly change our planet. Water creates clouds and weather, breaks down rocks, and helps balance the planet's temperature.

Water also runs the chemistry of life. Plants and animals need water to live and grow. Water makes up much of our bodies. If you weigh 75 pounds, your body has enough water to fill about eleven large soda bottles. All life needs water. Life and water go together.

Oceans are home to nearly 50 percent
of all species on earth.

Why is there life on Earth?

Earth is the only place where life has been found. It is also the only planet with liquid water on its surface. Water is a big reason life is here. On our neighbor planet Venus, all water boiled away because that planet is so close to the sun. Earth's distance from the sun is just right for life. Our other neighbor, Mars, is colder because it is farther from the sun. Mars is also cold because of its very thin atmosphere. The blanket of gas around a planet is its atmosphere. Earth's atmosphere also helps makes life possible. It holds in heat and blocks out dangerous rays from the sun.

Life showed up early in Earth's history. It sprang up once life-supporting conditions were here—liquid water, mild temperatures, and a suitable atmosphere. Life has existed on Earth for at least the last 3.5 billion years. Early life changed Earth's atmosphere. It put more oxygen into the air. This made Earth able to support more kinds of life, including animals. Life continues to change our planet. Plants make oxygen and break up rocks. Today, life of some sort exists nearly everywhere on Earth—land, water, and air. Even boiling hot springs and frozen lakes are home to tiny life-forms. Scientists think there could be as many as 8.7 million different species, or kinds, of living things on Earth.

A thin layer of gases, the atmosphere, wraps around Earth. It gives us air to breathe and protects the planet from the sun's dangerous rays.

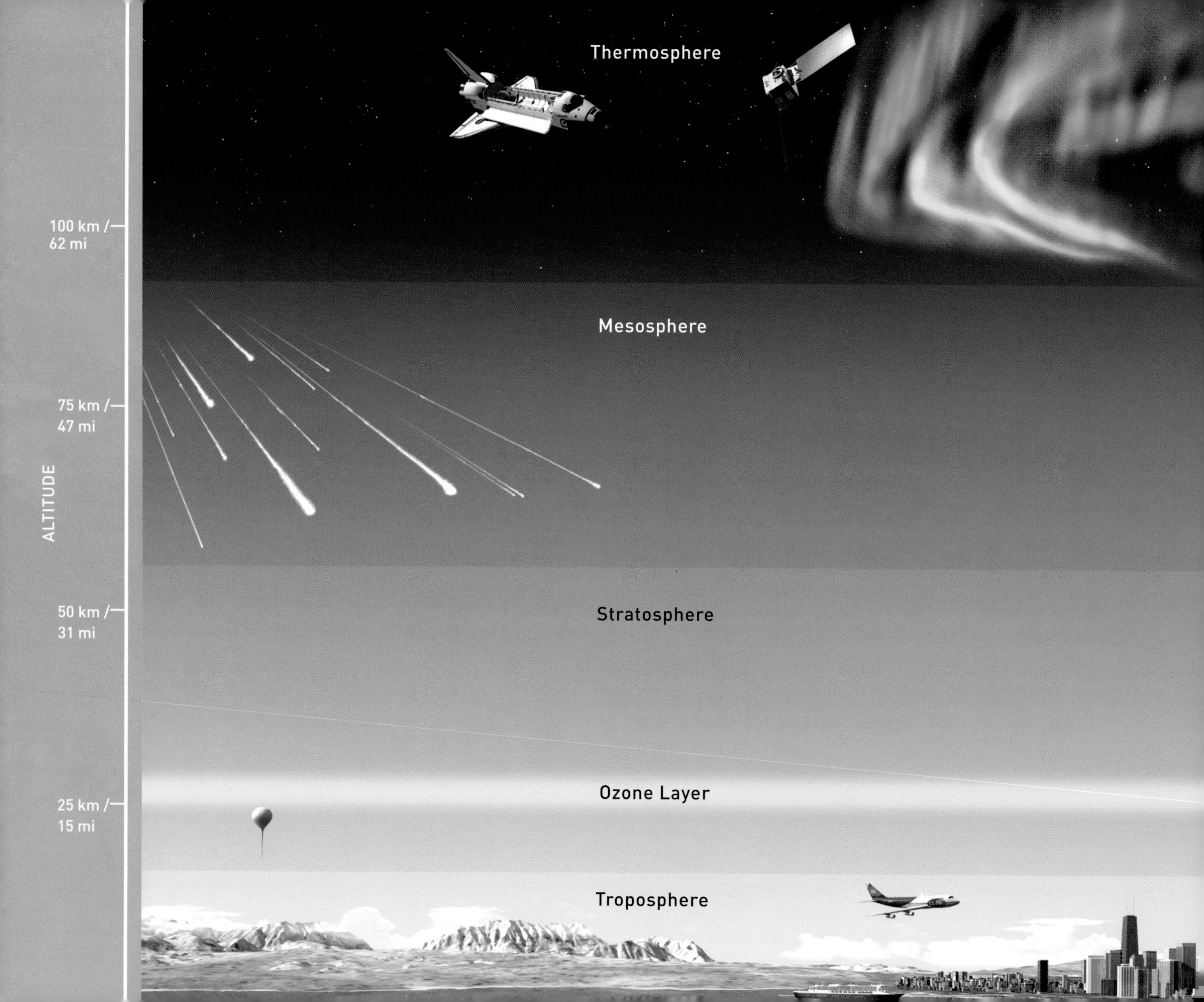

ALTITUDE

Thermosphere

100 km /
62 mi

Mesosphere

75 km /
47 mi

50 km /
31 mi

Stratosphere

Ozone Layer

25 km /
15 mi

Troposphere

Why is the sky blue?

Take a deep breath. You just breathed in some of Earth's atmosphere! The air between Earth's surface and outer space is called the atmosphere. Air is made up of different gases. Oxygen is the gas we need to power our bodies. But it is nitrogen gas that makes up more than three-fourths of our air. Nitrogen is also why the sky is blue. Sunlight bounces off nitrogen gas and scatters lots of blue light down toward us, so we see the sky as blue.

There is no blue sky out in space. Space starts about 60 miles (100 km) above Earth. There are still some gases beyond that, but not many. The atmosphere's gases are thickest at the surface but thin out the higher you go. You know this if you've ever climbed a mountain. There is less oxygen to breathe on mountaintops. Scientists divide the atmosphere into four main layers, from top to bottom. The layer nearest outer space is the thermosphere. This is where radio waves bounce around and colorful curtains of light called auroras ripple in bands of green, red, and blue. Below it is the mesosphere, where the air is not quite as thin. There are enough gases in the mesosphere to slow down and burn up meteors falling toward Earth. We see them as falling stars. The stratosphere is where the important ozone layer is. It protects us from dangerous solar rays. The lowest layer of the atmosphere is the troposphere. This is where breathable air is and where weather happens.

What creates our weather?

Earth's weather happens where the most air is. This is in the bottom layer of the atmosphere, the troposphere. The air here is always moving. The sun shines on the hills, oceans, and other surfaces of Earth. This heats up the air above them. Warm air is lighter than cold air, and so it rises. Warm air cools as it rises. The now cool air is heavy, and so it sinks back down. This constant up-and-down movement of air, driven by the sun, creates weather.

Weather is what is going on in the atmosphere at a specific place and time. Temperature is part of weather, and so is moving air, or wind. Water is the other basic weather ingredient besides air and sun. Earth's water is always moving between the surface and the air. Ocean water evaporates into the air and forms clouds that deliver rain and snow to faraway places. Clouds hold tons of water. A thunderstorm cloud holds as much water as what spills over Niagara Falls in six minutes. Weather helps move water from place to place.

Thunderstorm clouds grow into towering giants as warm, moist air rises inside them and adds more layers of dark, rain-filled clouds.

Why is the moon important to Earth?

Watching the moon change phases is a lot of fun. It goes from bright and full to a silvery sliver and back again. However, the moon is more than a lovely sight in the night sky. Earth would be a very different planet without it. The moon causes the water in oceans and large lakes to rise and fall each day—this is called the tide. The moon's pull on large bodies of water creates the tides. Tides go from low to high as the moon goes around Earth. The moon also keeps Earth from wobbling. Our moon helps lock in a steady orbit for our planet. This makes the seasons regular and the climate steady.

The moon can do all this because it's nearby and really big. It's large and heavy enough to affect Earth. How unusual is the moon? Lots of planets have moons. A moon is any space object that orbits a bigger space object. Giant Jupiter has more than sixty moons, and a few, such as Ganymede, are bigger than our moon. But our moon is quite large compared to the small size of Earth. Three of our moons lined up side by side would stretch nearly across Earth. It would take more than twenty-nine Ganymedes to stretch across Jupiter.

The moon is continually dragging ocean waters toward itself as it circles Earth every month. Daily tides happen as Earth spins on its axis and water is pulled toward the moon.

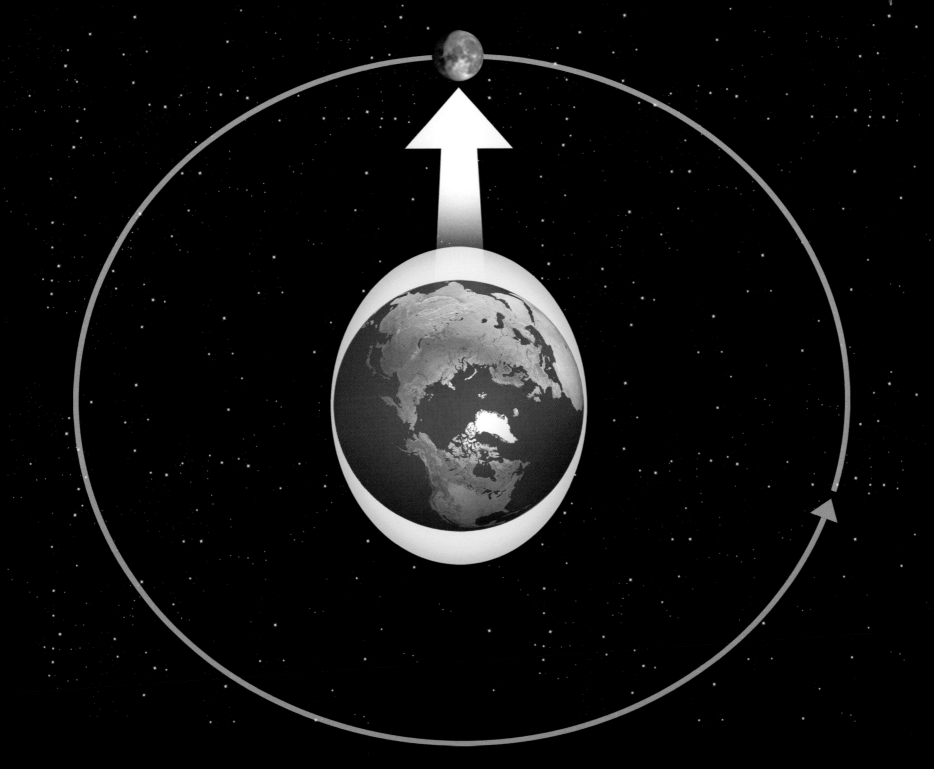

Why do we have seasons?

What time of year is it where you live? Is it summer or winter, spring or autumn? Earth, like the other planets, travels around the sun. The time it takes for Earth to make one orbit around the sun is one year. Why is part of the year warmer than other times? Because Earth is tilted. Earth's axis is not straight up and down—it's tilted. Imagine our planet as a ball of yarn with a knitting needle stuck through it. The ball of yarn would spin around with the knitting needle leaning a bit to the side.

Earth's tilted axis means that different parts of the planet get different amounts of sunlight. During part of Earth's orbit around the sun, the North Pole tips toward the sun. The top half of the planet gets more sunlight and has summer. Meanwhile, the bottom half of Earth tilts away from the sun, gets less sunlight, and has winter. Six months later Earth is on the other side of the sun. Then the South Pole tips toward the sun, and the bottom half of the planet gets more sunlight and has summer. Meanwhile, the top half has winter.

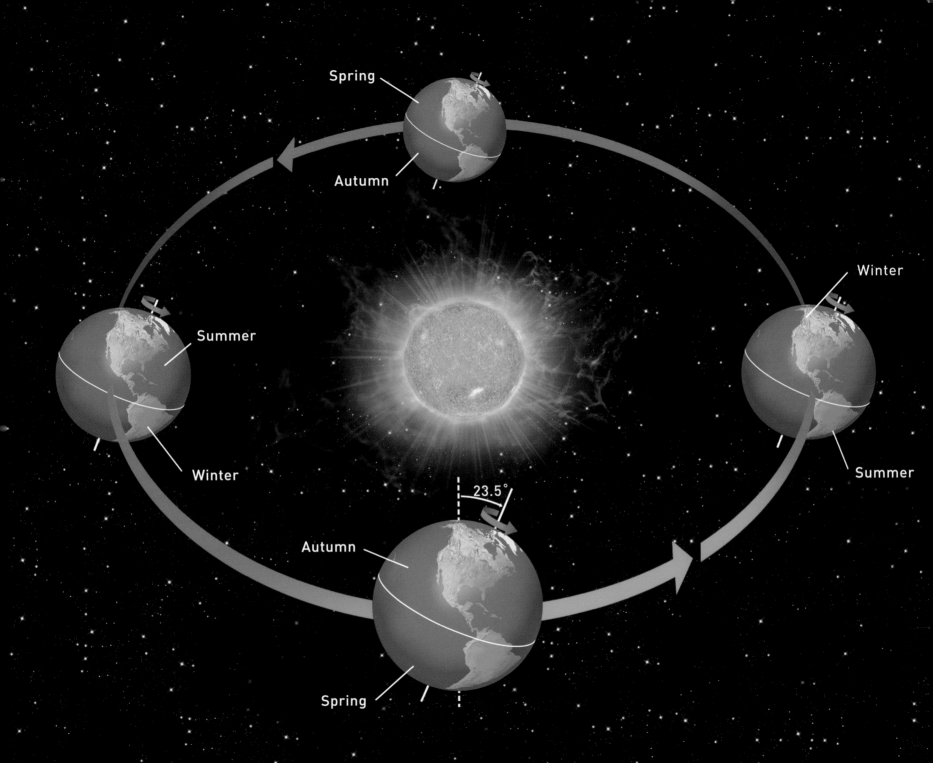

Lut Desert is a large salt desert in southeastern Iran. It has some of the tallest sand dunes in the world.

What is the hottest place on Earth?

Deserts are the hottest places on the planet. A desert is a dry, bare place where it doesn't rain much, plants are few, and wildlife is limited. About a third of Earth's land is desert. All deserts are dry, but only some are hot. The hottest deserts are the ones that soak up the most sunlight. They are in countries near the equator where the directly overhead sun hits the land like a spotlight. Australia, North Africa, southern China, and Mexico have some of the hottest deserts. The very hottest? Lut Desert in Iran wins with a highest overall temperature of 159.3°F (70.7°C).

The Soviet Union founded Antarctica's Vostok Station in 1957. Today, scientists from all over the world do research there.

What is the coldest place on Earth?

Odd as it seems, the coldest spot on Earth is also a desert. Much of Antarctica gets very little snow and has few lakes or rivers, no plants, and few animals. The Vostok science station near the South Pole measured the record coldest temperature of –128.6°F (–89.2°C). Brrrr! What are the runners-up for the coldest location? The North Pole, Greenland, and Siberia can have temperatures as low as –90°F (–68°C). On a February day in Siberia, one weather scientist tossed boiling water from a cup into the air. It froze into snow before hitting the ground!

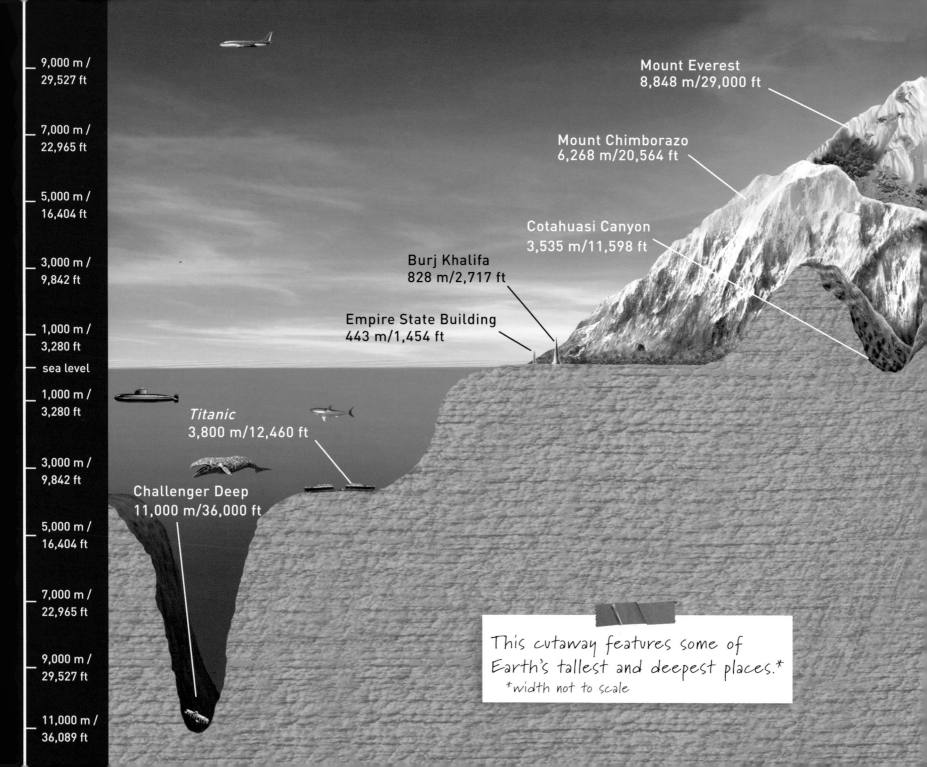

9,000 m / 29,527 ft

7,000 m / 22,965 ft

5,000 m / 16,404 ft

3,000 m / 9,842 ft

1,000 m / 3,280 ft

sea level

1,000 m / 3,280 ft

3,000 m / 9,842 ft

5,000 m / 16,404 ft

7,000 m / 22,965 ft

9,000 m / 29,527 ft

11,000 m / 36,089 ft

Mount Everest
8,848 m/29,000 ft

Mount Chimborazo
6,268 m/20,564 ft

Cotahuasi Canyon
3,535 m/11,598 ft

Burj Khalifa
828 m/2,717 ft

Empire State Building
443 m/1,454 ft

Titanic
3,800 m/12,460 ft

Challenger Deep
11,000 m/36,000 ft

This cutaway features some of Earth's tallest and deepest places.*
*width not to scale

What is the highest place on Earth?

Mountains are the highest places on the planet. The tallest mountain is Mount Everest at more than 29,000 feet (8,848 meters) high. That's nearly up where jet airliners fly. As if it that wasn't tall enough, it's still growing! Mount Everest is part of the Himalayas Mountains. They are continually pushed up by the forces that created them—India's tectonic plate is pushing against the Eurasian Plate and shoving it higher and higher. The Himalayas continue to rise about an inch (2 cm) a year.

Mount Everest is the tallest mountain, but it is not the farthest from the center of Earth. A mountain in Ecuador, called Chimborazo, is that winner. How is that possible? Earth is not a perfectly round sphere. It is a bit fatter around its middle, like a slightly squashed orange. Although Everest is taller, Mount Chimborazo is 1½ miles (2.5 km) closer to outer space. Which do you think should be crowned "the highest"?

What is the deepest place on Earth?

When you think of deep places, canyons come to mind. Cotahuasi Canyon in southwestern Peru is Earth's deepest. It is more than 2 miles (about 3.5 km) down to its bottom. That's twice as deep as the Grand Canyon in Arizona.

There are deeper places in Earth's crust, however. Where? In the great deep itself—the ocean. The deepest part of the ocean is under the western Pacific Ocean halfway between Japan and New Guinea. Here lies Challenger Deep, a narrow slot-shaped canyon in the seafloor. At a depth of at least 6½ miles (11 km), it's the deepest place known. If Mount Everest were sunk down inside Challenger Deep, more than 1 mile (1.5 km) of ocean would cover its peak.

What does an Earth scientist study?

Earth scientists study Earth and its place in the universe. That covers a lot! Most Earth scientists concentrate on one subject. If you study rocks and minerals, you are a geologist. Geologists learn about Earth's history by looking at rocks. A geologist might look for oil or try to predict when a volcano will erupt. A type of Earth science that tries to predict the weather is meteorology. How do meteorologists see into the future? How do they know if it will be sunny or rainy? They take measurements of the atmosphere's temperature, winds, and gases. Meteorologists also track storms, predict where the danger will be, and send out weather warnings to communities.

Oceans are a huge part of our planet, and they have their own Earth science called oceanography. Oceanographers study all parts of the oceans—water, seafloor, and sea life. Believe it or not, part of Earth science is what's beyond Earth! Astronomers study stars, planets, moons, comets, and other space stuff. They are constantly learning more about how our small terrestrial ocean planet fits into the cosmos.

Earth scientists that study volcanoes are called volcanologists. This one is studying Mount Yasur on Tanna Island in the South Pacific.

FIND OUT MORE

Books to Read

Carson, Mary Kay. *Far-Out Guide to Earth*. Berkeley Heights, NJ: Enslow, 2010.

Ride, Sally, and Tam O'Shaughnessy. *Mission: Planet Earth: Our World and Its Climate—and How Humans Are Changing Them*. New York: Flash Point/Roaring Brook Press, 2009.

Snedden, Robert. *Mapping Earth from Space*. Chicago: Heinemann-Raintree, 2011.

Solway, Andrew. *Why Is There Life on Earth?* Chicago: Heinemann-Raintree, 2011.

Taylor, Barbara. *Navigators: Planet Earth*. New York: Kingfisher, 2012.

Turner, Pamela S. *Life on Earth—and Beyond: An Astrobiologist's Quest*. Watertown, MA: Charlesbridge, 2008.

Websites to Visit

EARTH OBSERVATORY
http://earthobservatory.nasa.gov
Check out amazing satellite pictures and maps of our planet.

EPA CLIMATE CHANGE KIDS SITE
http://epa.gov/climatechange/kids/
Read and learn about climate change.

FOR KIDS ONLY: EARTH SCIENCE
http://kids.earth.nasa.gov/
Learn about land, water, air, and natural hazards and play Earth science games, too.

INDEX